# The Wallflower
# That Bloomed

# The Wallflower
# That Bloomed

Catherine C. Berquin

ISBN: 1973947684
ISBN 13: 9781973947684

# Contents

*To my mother, who has been my rock and pillow.*
*To my papa, who has been my best friend always.*
*To my nana, whose love caresses my soul.*

*Thank you...*
*I am all that I am because of you.*

*And as grateful as I am to all the souls who have taught*
*me lessons, this one's for me...*

*...finally learning to love myself.*

We carved love letters into our arms
And prayers into our thighs

Asked God to take us back and save us all at the same time
I think she got confused.

# Chapter 1
# Womanhood Is Not a
# Synonym for Censorship

My heart stopped belonging to me a while ago;
my body was never auctioned.

My petals were stolen, and nobody wanted my thorns.
"Be more ladylike"
was always the cause of her storm.

I craved your dominance—unaware—it came with a dog tag as cold as my ancestor's shackles.

Release me.

As "Damn" rolled off his tongue and shivers spiraled down my spine, I felt his eyelashes flutter against my nipple as he imagined himself kissing stolen property.

The way his mind had allowed him to steal my breath and all the gold beneath, I used mine to steal time…rewinding. Pausing his "Damn" and reversing the truck that passed by. When I pressed play he would open his mouth, and halfway through "Da—" the truck would hit the brakes and him all alike, and I would never experience the chills of this strange man on my walk to the train again.

But society would tell you I was the criminal, so I flush with embarrassment instead. Knowing I'll be met with more for the remaining blocks to come.

# Chapter 2
# The Breakup

Undeserving.

I anticipated your heart shattering into a million pieces, and so I threw mine into the cross fires. I allowed you to break me— to keep yourself—and still there are parts of you, you won't take home.

Unforgiving. Please take all of you.

Thank you; don't come again.

I wondered why you couldn't love me, why I was not good
enough. If I hadn't loved hard enough or if I had loved too
hard. Was I your sugar or your salt?

Salt is what danced around the glasses of acid you drank to
forget me. Sugar is what you'd never once again taste.

I was worthy.
I know that,
now.

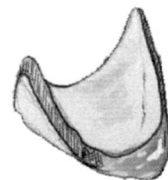

They didn't teach me how to love you
Excuse number one
And there's an orchestra playing at the beat of my heart while my eyes
pour you wine
It's OK; we can learn together
They didn't hug me often or hold my hand; I don't know affection
Excuse number two
And there's memories of all the love I've nearly drowned in flooding
my mind till all my soul can do is share it and hope you don't mind
They never told me that they loved me
Excuse number three
And love has now become my favorite word, "I love you" my favorite
phrase
"I need you" echoes through my soul
You'll feel me
My peanut-butter lips latching on to you like the end of a balloon
I'll fill you till I'm empty
I don't regret you
Haven't you learned yet?
This is what love is

They didn't teach me how to love you
Excuse number one
My soul wants us to learn together
With clavicles colliding
And Erykah Badu filling the airwaves
With no substance clouding our clouded judgment
My mind understands that you are not my puppet; I cannot
pull at your strings

You are not my child; I cannot teach you love
I can give you love and hope that my love is so strong it forces itself into
you and takes over you

Till I'm your first and last thought when you close your eyes
Till your wet dreams create new oceans because I've taught you with
my lips on you, every inch of you is now your spot
They didn't hug me often or hold my hand; I don't know affection
Excuse number two
And my soul hugs you
It squeezes you so tight your skin unzips and your soul is free
My lips meet your forehead embracing sexuality and sensuality, ex-
pressing innocence and vulgarity
As my fingers caress your spine
They never told me that they loved me
Excuse number three
Love pours out of me
Too much love pours out of me
My soul thinks not enough love poured out of me but it killed you
Stifled in a love you've never felt
Three excuses, one death, and a broken heart later, I considered laying
both sets of these lips in the midst of a soul as cold
as the one I used to own
But there's no ice that could tame this fire

I'm craving warmth.

My lips latching on to you
Spewing proverbs
Singing psalms
There's no book for us
So we write our own...

...The essence of poetry:
Love and liberty

The brokenhearted can't relate.

We'd soon learn, we can't relate.

You wanted me broken

I'm now unhinged
Melting in the hands of anyone who can tell me what I really am.

I cried for you
I didn't taste the ocean this time
I think my eyes were just full
There were no waves
This stream led me to dry land
Where all salt turns to sugar

Release...

# Chapter 3
# …For a Black Girl

To my daughter:
I love the way I've imagined you—created in my image.
I've seen an Afro full of tight-knit curls, dark skin,
long lashes, some hips, and dreams of ass every time I've
thought of you.

I'm just hoping you'll love it too.

"If you were lighter, you'd be beautiful."

If only he knew my soul was a replica of the sun, my mind was a galaxy, and he was unworthy.

To my future son,

Every time I imagine the natural birth I've planned for you, the image is tainted with scores of red. I squeeze my eyes a little tighter to fully embrace your skin with high doses of melanin, and constantly I'm met with red. Red circles, embracing the target you are, red embracing the blood I can expect you to shed, red embracing the anger I'll hold. I love you already, but your birth is what scares me. I'm nervous to birth my best friend and lose him. This world doesn't love you, but I promise I do. I'm battling in my mind how to compromise. Feeling like it's either you never come or I say goodbye. Just a figment of my imagination, and already my heart breaks. Too many of your brothers have allowed their innocence to take them away. Have they allowed their innocence to take them away? I apologize; that was ignorant. A system so corrupt has broken the backs of our kings; they've placed weights on our minds and told us we couldn't stand.

To my future son,

Your existence doesn't scare me; it inspires me. My thoughts were stifled for just a minute, but now I'm operating on free cognition. I love you. The world needs you. Another black king, my future black king, my baby boy. On your first day I'll embrace you; on your second day I'll embrace you; on all your days I'll embrace you. I'll teach you self-love and acceptance, respect and etiquette. I'll remind you how to carry yourself in every setting and that whatever contributes to the unique boy you are should never be stifled. I'll teach you to stand strong, but still I'll share my fears. I'll tell you what my world is like and pray yours ain't the same.

To my future son,

I plan to love you with every inch of me, and I pray that saves you from an early grave. Lord, I pray that that's enough…

My skin—the darkest part of me—is the silk cloth
wrapping God unveiled me in.

To him I was not just beautiful
See, I meant so much less, making my beauty that much more riveting
I wasn't inhumane, but for lack of better words, I guess he found me unhuman
Pitied my existence
And ridiculed my blood for emulating the redness of his
To him I was not just beautiful
I was toasted skin melted on broken bones
I was indecent exposure
Arrest me
To him I was not just beautiful
I was the Pocahontas to his John Smith
A warrior
Not quite a woman
But not a man either
Meant for sex but not worthy of reproduction
Exotic but not intoxicating
I was the thorn on the rose, the demise of society
To him I was not just beautiful, I was confusion
I was mischief
I was the embodiment of poverty, disgrace, stupidity, ghettos, hunger, and Ebonics
To him I was not just beautiful
Rather I was not beautiful enough
I held one too many kinks in the hair I refuse to perm
Far too many pounds in the lips I part when speaking
My curves existed and my eyes were dark

The sun didn't rip at my melanin
To him I was not just beautiful
I was beautiful for a black girl

I was beautiful despite all he imagined I could afford
for breakfast was honey and rice

I had grace despite the fact that my people came from the pits; I had
humor and understood joy despite the fact that my people were raped,
beaten, and enslaved for me to experience these days
I knew what it meant to read, to write, and to teach
I knew beauty for self-acceptance

See, to him I was not just beautiful
I was beautiful for a black woman
A story untold, unheard of...
To him I was everything society said I couldn't be.
He couldn't accept all that I was without painting a white woman over
me

To him I'll never be just beautiful.

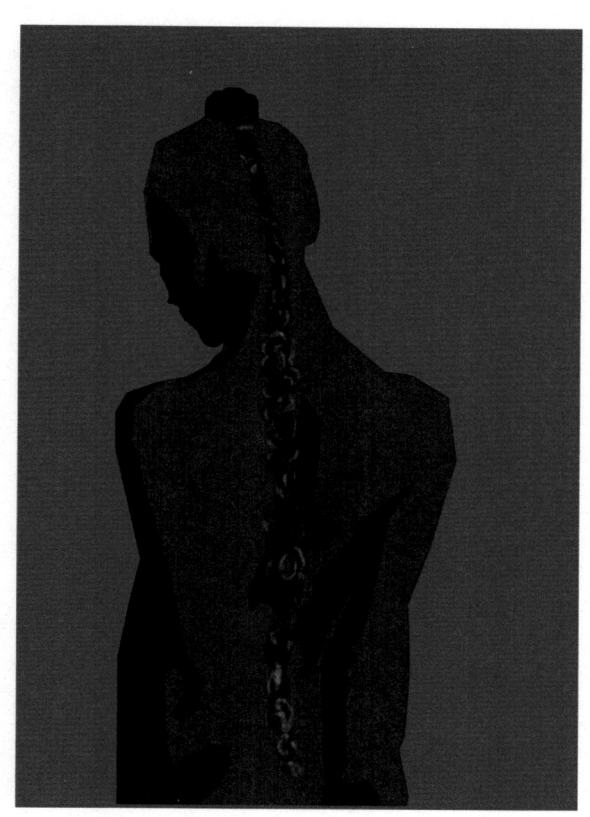

# Chapter 4
# I Don't Love You...

I live inside the minute, no, the second, well, the millisecond or half a second or second of a second of a second, whatever that may be called—I live in that moment before our first kiss where I felt you in my groin. Almost nauseous, the passion hit me with a trembling soul, my worries forgotten...I hadn't found a new home but a shelter—somewhere new to lay my head while the rain poured. The skies were gray far too long, and like a fly to a flame, I couldn't resist you...
With cupped hands I planned to drink from you; with an arched back I planned to feed you; with a closed heart I planned to never love you. With a naive soul you planned to fix me.

I don't think this will work.

I wanted so much, for us to be so much less than two souls blending.

I wanted our bodies to clash.

I planned to forget you.

I almost left my heart here

In the palm of your hand

But I knew if I had—it'd be misplaced before I needed it next.

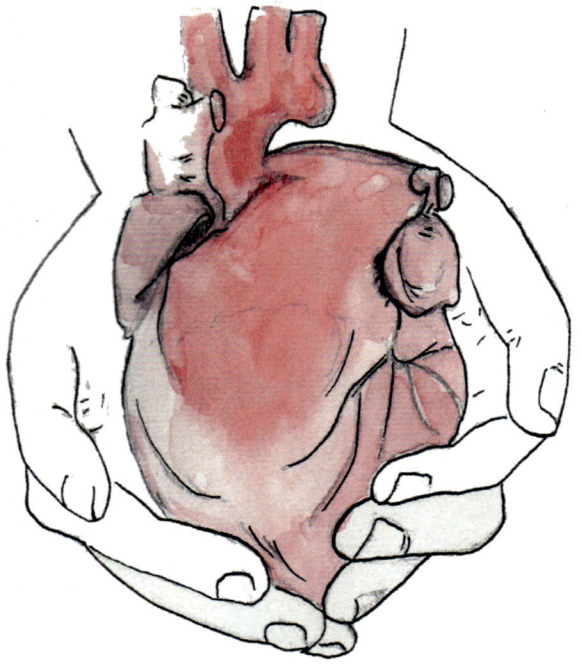

She said she wanted to make love. Yet, she hadn't realized my tongue'd performed a C-section, unveiling her soul—setting it free while forcing her to watch it cling to me. I'm sure she didn't fancy that caramel kisses would start a fire within, and that every time I pulled away, there'd be a line of ash for her to remember the last time she inhaled me. I bet she hadn't envisioned thinking of me every time she walked away, but the way my hands sunk to her head and stuck like a crown, there was no one else to think of. I don't think she knew how deep I'd plant myself, that'd I'd lay roots across her insides. She wasn't aware that every time her tongue grazed her lips she'd taste me, or that I'd be the reason for her teeth sensually holding on to her bottom lip. But she said she wanted to make love, so we did...

# Chapter 5
# Seeds

Thighs spread. Praying,
"Lord, just let me break even."

Years later and the pieces don't fit together;
how many ways can we interpret no?

I felt the demons crawl out of him and into me

Who do I belong to now?

Praying for blue skies

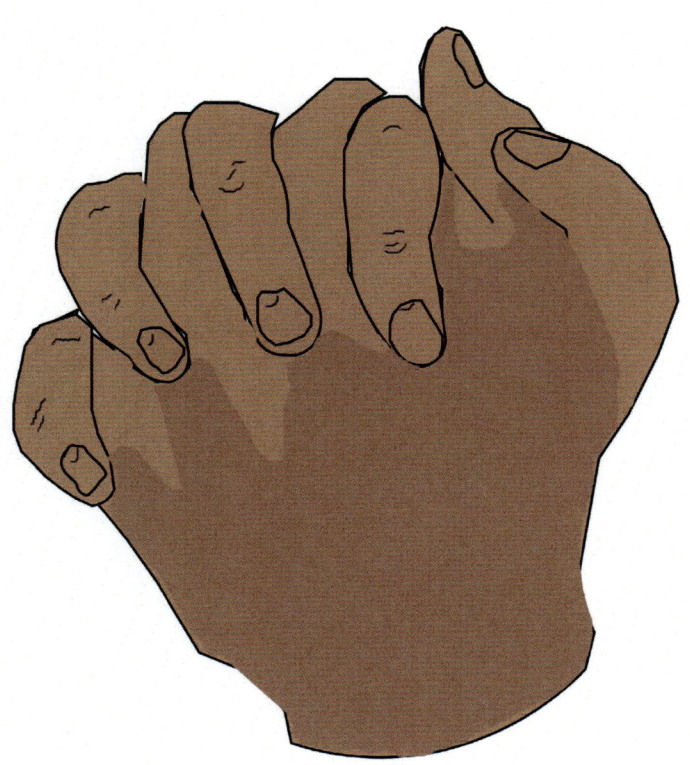

I've often wondered how the apology would sound.

Would I recognize the groveling? The way your mouth curved out of sorrow, would I know it immediately or would it be as strange as you and I in that bed? Would you apologize for "the act" too ashamed to name it, unable to fully come to peace with knowing your cum broke me to pieces. Would you apologize for believing your manhood made me all woman and then blame how submissive your mother always was? Would you tell me that you misheard each time no bounced from my lips to the wall? That when I closed my legs and begged for you to stop only to be forced wide open you misread the signs? Would it make both of us survivors of a wild night ? Or would you dig the pieces of me from under your nails and mail them home?

I've often wondered if the apology would make me whole.

I ran home to run the water
Scratch him off of me
Scream in an empty house
Listen to the echoes and make sense out of why no one came to my
rescue
Drown my pities with my existence in this shower
And when that fails swallow too many pills to make it
And when my consciousness prevails
Call and tell whoever will listen that I need help, that I need them
That I'm tainted
I'm unlovable
I'm stolen goods, no one could regift me
They wouldn't want to
Call and tell them that I'm lonely and I'm dying and he raped me
Call and tell them that I don't know who I am, who this body belongs
to but I need to escape it
Call and tell them that I can't get out of this body
That I'm alone in this house and he's still on top of me
That I tried to drown in the shower
That I've taken too many pills
That nothing is working we're all still here
My shadow and his demons
All still lurking
Call and tell them that I don't know how to properly kill myself
That I don't know how to properly kill him
That I don't know anything
All I can see is him raping me

All I hear is myself screaming, crying, gagging and then in the moments that my body stops to breathe I hear the slow hands of the clock louder than the creak of the bed
Call and tell them that I've banged my head against the wall with hopes I'd forget
Call and tell them that I finally fought in the shower the way I should've fought all along
Call and tell them that someone needs to be here to hug me, to hold me
Call and tell them that I'm not sure I'd even let anyone get close but I just need a friend
Call and tell them when I scream I need someone to save me, to hear me

I ran home hoping someone could see me.

"Boys will be boys"—the epitome of my silence

I still haven't forgiven myself for the day you ripped my clothes off and
kept my legs spread as I begged God to save me and stared at the clock
for solace

They said I can
They said I should
Forgive myself

For the rounds of bullets I imagined flying into you
And the God I imagined killing you
And the blades I wore as bracelets
And the pills I knew were not candy

They said I can
They said I should
Forgive myself

For not having stronger legs and a louder cry
For praying for the moment's end and not justice
For letting you roam

They said I can
They said I should
Forgive myself

For taking this long to reclaim stolen property
For not loving this skin more
For wanting to shed instead of grow

They said I can forgive myself
They said I should
As if I purposely close my eyes to the sounds of screams muted by
clocks and the smell of alcohol
They said I can, they said I should forgive myself
For all the years I thought it was okay

At first I thought I should've opened the door
If I had just let you in, it wouldn't be a robbery
You wouldn't have gotten all around town with my innermost secrets
My wet secreting in the palm of your unforgiven hands
My vulva throbbing against your underdeveloped penis
At first I thought I should've opened the door because I felt weak
knowing you unlocked it anyway
Because I was ashamed
Because the word rape won't only hurt your reputation but mine
At first I thought maybe I'll just tell the world this is what I wanted
Then I learned that my self-love was too overbearing to allow pity, self-
blame, or shame
I didn't unlock the door, and you breaking in somehow made me stron-
ger but still...
No, thank you

I bit my lip in response to the question he never asked
Bit it till it bled
My legs danced badly
My stomach hurled itself into backflips
And my heels banged themselves together in a homesick rage
My back arched in defeat
As my vagina secreted tears
My voice became an empty well
My fingers trembled
And my skin crawled

He thrusted.

And then finally he said is this okay?

No.

Dear Reader,

Thank you for for allowing me the freedom to share the ugliest parts of myself. For allowing me to feel beautiful and naked in this text. For allowing me to cry, to scream, to laugh, to smile in the palm of your hands. Thank you for picking up this piece of my heart, for allowing my story to be told and if you can relate to any of it thank you for not giving up. Thank you for remaining strong with me and continuing to build.

I love you all, I appreciate you.

I am honored and I am grateful.

Love,

The Wallflower

Made in the USA
San Bernardino, CA
18 June 2018